WARRIOR WI

WARRIOR WISDOM SUN

WARRIOR WISDOM SUN

WARRIOR WISDOM SUN

Poems on battle, lessons and liberation

SARAH ELLIOTT

BRIGHTEST LIGHT PUBLISHING HOUSE

WARRIOR WISDOM SUN

BRIGHTEST
LIGHT

BRIGHTEST LIGHT PUBLISHING HOUSE

Copyright © 2022 Sarah Elliott

All rights reserved. No part of this publication may be reproduced, distributed, or transmitted in any form by any means, including photocopying, recording, or other electronic methods without the prior written permission of the author, except in the case of brief quotations embodied in reviews and certain other non-commercial uses permitted by copyright law.

ISBN: 978-1-7396808-0-0

DEDICATION

To Mum and Dad and the ancestors long passed; you are where my journey began. Gratitude, admiration and love to you always.

For the Divine within me and for those yet to come.

WARRIOR WISDOM SUN

CONTENTS

1	Introduction	1
2	Warrior	Pg 4
3	Wisdom	Pg 73
4	Sun	Pg 113
5	Spoken Word	Pg 133
6	Acknowledgements	Pg 162

WARRIOR WISDOM SUN

INTRODUCTION

So here we are reader. Maybe you chose to read this book because you felt that something resonated. Maybe it was a recommendation. Maybe you don't even know why. Whichever, I am glad that you did. We are all separate but connected. We all share a spectrum of emotions; apart yet together.

These writings chronicle my journey through difficult times. They give a voice to the emotions I felt inside rather than having them deeply submerged or raging like a monster. Maybe I could give The Hulk some tips! Awareness of my thoughts and feelings helps me to accept. By accept, I don't mean rolling over and being passive, I mean simply allowing them to be - an acknowledgment of the reality. No longer do my emotions always decide my course of action and increasingly, instead of reacting, I am able to respond from a place of intuition.

This book is an opportunity to share my journey through the tumultuous terrains of life. It's not all doom and gloom though! The challenges are there but also the hard learnt lessons which (eventually) bring me back to reclaiming freedom. So much is in perception. It's like flicking through the various filters on social media until you find one that fits you at that moment, in that incarnation. You can always go back and change it; there is no penalty. And that is one of the things I have learned through this process. There is no penalty. No penalty when I get things wrong, when I don't understand, or even if I change my mind completely!

This therapeutic process has brought me to joy, liberation and love. Love for the self. Acceptance. Unconditional. It's a complicated journey and sometimes I trip, I fall, I go round in circles and I go back and take a path I've already taken. But I'm ok with that now. It's my journey.

You never see it when you're right in the thick of it all, just surviving, putting on a brave face and trying to get on with things. When you step back, allow yourself space and truly see, you can be astounded at what the truth of a situation is once you tear away the programming. Everyone's journey is different and we travel at our own pace, taking or leaving behind what we will and meeting many others on the way. I am grateful for you meeting me here. Thank you.

Sarah

WARRIOR

The voices are so loud today

a cacophony of sound

clashing

screeching

disharmony

whirling in my head

deafening me

blocking out all the good things

I worked so hard to gain

the voices are screaming to me

the lies they scream at me

you're not enough, they're better, who do you think you are, you're no good, you're too fat,

you're too thin, you're too ugly, you're too stupid, you're not intelligent enough,

you're not beautiful enough, you can't do that, you can't do that!

the voices are screaming today

so I pick up my remote and I press mute

I pick up my remote and I press mute

I pick up my remote and I press mute

because I am in control

I have the remote

I can choose

I have the remote

I can choose

whether to visit the past

stay in the present

plan in the future

I have the remote

and I can choose

I can pause and sit with the picture

enjoy the present

without fast forwarding to the future

and going on and on and on

and worrying about what may be

or rewinding back to the past

and re-visiting and re-visiting

and remembering and remembering

and regretting

and worrying about what I could've done

should've done must've done

but didn't

I have the remote

and I can stay with the present

I can enjoy the present

I can mute the voices

I can increase the volume

and hear the truth that is being spoken to me

I have the remote

I have the control

I have the choice. -----

That elusive shiny thing

that

Seems to flit in and out

like

Willo the Wisp

We chase it

Hoping, dreaming

Wishing, wanting

Aching, yearning

When we finally have it

Our joy is short lived

The ecstasy fades

We worry about losing it

How we will be without it

Forgetting we existed

Without it

In the first place. -----

The knight in shining armour

The charming prince

The fantasy ever after

Has so long since

Slipped secretly away

Or torn and ripped out

Can't learn the lesson

What is love about?

Not what they told

Nor what I saw

Or heard or read

In books galore

Ever changing, so confusing

The lies I'm told

Are not amusing

Watch their actions

Not their words

Advice I'm given

But still can't learn

These many difficult

Challenging lessons

Hurtful at times

Not feeling like blessings

Yet I continue ever climbing

Trying to touch that

Silver lining. -----

At first I was prized

Shiny, innovative and new

A break from the past

The familiar boring, expected

Kept safe up high

But oh so often chosen

Again and again

Enjoyed

Consumed

Devoured

Then not picked up so often

No longer first choice

My shine had diminished

Looking a little worn now

Cover torn and crumpled

Others chosen before me

No longer on trend

On show

Or on point

Colours withdrawing

Creases appearing

Don't they know

I can still satisfy

Be of worth

Fulfil a need

Empower

Support

Sometimes nostalgia will lift me down

But always short lived

More and more time up here now

Left on the shelf. -----

When you clench your fist

in frustration

in rage

in anger

When you curl and claw your fingers

grasping in greed

holding onto fear

Your hands are no longer open to receiving

Release

Release

Release

Stretch out your palms

and fingers

in gratitude

and expectation. -----

The past is a hotel

we visited it fleetingly

it was home for a while

it may have been 5*

it may not

but we're not there right now

we were there

we've been

we don't need to go back

the future is a newbuild full of possibilities

ideas, plans shifting, changing, subject to

change beyond our control

but we're not there right now

we are here

home

and it feels good

why do we leave so often

return. -----

Oh it'll do

it will not do

don't you see

these words aren't true

why settle for less

you'll end in a mess

don't underrate

don't second guess

you deserve more

your life is natural

re-examine your thoughts

be confident and sure. -----

It takes courage to acknowledge vulnerability

It takes bravery to share it

It takes more than you think you have to navigate it

It takes utter and complete conviction to know you will come through it

What a superhero you are. -----

You don't have to accept

every offer

who taught you

it wasn't polite or good

or right or kind

to decline

to say no

to pass

to defer to reject

you may have many offers

you may have one

you will always have

the choice

not to accept

not to offer an explanation

not to feel obliged

bound by duty

by expectations

who wants to be bound

step back

be circumspect

see the truth

decide, decline

if needed

on

your

own

terms

It might feel uncomfortable

when you decline

an invitation

an opportunity

an offer of advice

it might feel uncomfortable

when you decide

not to return that call

not to do the chores

not to do that favour

it might feel uncomfortable

when you choose

to skip working out

to have a lie in

to put yourself first

it might feel uncomfortable

initially

until it feels easy. -----

Just because

you didn't lose your home

you didn't experience violence

you didn't have bereavement

just because

you're not a recovering addict

you're not a cancer survivor

you're not...

doesn't mean you haven't

had to

fight

be brave

work through your trauma

try and fail and try again

experience the

dark

empty

cold

shadows

you have also found courage

started again

and have a voice

a story to share

just because. -----

Forgiveness

almost like a legend

steeped in truth

but embellished

the topic of discussion

an idea

something desired

partially understood

intellectually grasped

but hard to implement

so needed

so essential

graced to others

and for others

but for self?

forgiveness

the legend continues. -----

Sometimes I just want

to take a break

step down from the stage

of perfection

pull off the wig

of positivity

remove the make up

of selflessness

peel off the costume

of always being right

kick off the boots

of being good

and reveal

the nakedness

the purity

the truth

the reality

the me

sometimes. -----

The smell has faded

from the scarf she wore

but your warm hugs linger

the sound of your soft voice

a memory echo now

but your kind words remain

the warmth of your smile

no longer brightens the room

but the glow of

your love remains

your charm

your grace

your thoughtfulness

your generosity

your sense of fun

your love touched so many

I miss you

so much

mum.

*written when I had a cold and I just wanted my mum -----

A line from the film

A father daughter hug

on screen

makes me ask

why

why couldn't you

stay long enough

so we could have

more hugs

why

why did you go without

creating more memories

hearing you say

I love you

holding me like a

lost little girl

I felt so lost

when you left

so broken

so empty

without purpose

I wanted to see that sparkle in your eye

hear the questions you used to ask

the stories of home

you would tell

your deep singing voice

your laugh

your cakes

your banana fritters

your patties

your generosity

your love

dad. -----

So tired of loss

And angry

So sad of losing

My loved ones

So fed up

Of funerals, eulogies

Cemeteries, coffins and tears

So over being strong

Supporting everyone but

Me

I have lost so much

With no space to grieve

No time, no energy

It's no wonder

I find it hard

To let go, release

Even when holding on

Is bad for me

Grasping at

Toxic, rotten, foul

Things

That bring me down

So scared of loss

The experience too hard

Too familiar

Too often

But I know and I am

Learning

To let go

To grieve

To make space

For the divine things

The good things

Peace, joy and love

My entitlement

My birthright

My being. -----

I knew that

they would pass

these uncomfortable

feelings

the ones that

plague your thoughts

crawl under your skin

obscure your vision

kidnap your voice

and leave you

paralysed

motionless

still as stone

and just as cold

empty

heavy

immovable

I knew that

they would pass

but I still

didn't want them there

I didn't want

to sit

in the dark

cold

silent

empty

reminding myself

that I had been

here before

visited often really

and always

escaped

emerged

evolved

I knew that

they would pass

and I would be

wiser

stronger

elevated

and if they came

visiting again

I would be so full

there would be

little room

for them to stay

very long

so they can just

pass

off. -----

And so I find

My courage

My light

My knowledge

My truth

So I can live

Free

In each moment

A breath, a step

A moment

At a time. -----

Trauma

it happened

it's still here

an imprint

a programme

running in the background

of my system

but I'm still here too

I control the program

I can make it

meet my needs

trauma

I'm not here

because of you

Nor despite you

I'm just here

trauma

you happened

I am aware

I accept

But I am still

the one

who decides. -----

Why so hard to let go?

you hold on so tight

water runs through

your fingers

so easily finding a way

let whatever you are

holding onto

be like water

let it flow

trickle

drip

evaporate

and leave you

with an

empty hand

ready to receive. -----

Habits can be hard

to stop or change

or introduce

it's a patience piece

we have to be

kind to ourselves

and slow

slow like molasses

in January

dragging like the last minute

before the bell rings

slow motion

it takes control

and strength

and perseverance

conviction

and a clear goal

ahead. -----

When you're absent

from something or someone

for a while

things change

shifting unrecognisable

maybe derelict

uncared for

neglected lost

and forgotten

don't be absent

from you

for too long

check in

it might be

uncomfortable

at first

until you become

familiar again. -----

Fighting dragons

in my sleep

slaying monsters

and trying to keep

from falling further

deep and down

endlessly rolling

until I hit or lose my crown

I awake aching

stiff neck and back

tight shoulders

feeling filled with lack

what happens when

I fall asleep

drifting into slumber

the secrets I keep. -----

I falter

I pause

I wobble

fear unbalances me

wants to topple me

it's hard

staying balanced

like a feather

in a whirlwind

whipped around

out of control

I long for the calm

so I can drift along

under control

or in control

the uncertainty

throws me

battered and bruised

I feel

flung forward

batted back

twisted upward

slammed down

lightning strikes

divides the sky

shake things up

toppling towers

and when the

rubble calms

the dust settles

I remain

Steadfast. -----

The shock

disbelief

denial

distress

the news of

an elder passing

grief gets no easier

flashbacks

of fond childhood memories

guilt at

not having visited

more often

spiralling back

to old programmes

lies and untruths

about never putting

yourself first

always doing

what is seen as

right and good

no matter the loss

to your well-being

a myriad

of emotions

an overwhelming

tsunami

but you have

survived many tsunamis

find your lifejacket

no lifejacket

remember you can float

you will resurface

and if you need to take

a breath to go under

fine

come up when

you are ready

it's your own timing.-----

When the elders

march on

into the mist

and you lose sight

of them

it feels like they

take a part of you

your childhood

your innocence and joy

your safety net

know that

there is always

change

rebirth

transformation

the past

is still there

it cannot be erased

don't dwell there too long

or you will miss

the present

ground yourself in the now

connect to the truth

they may be

beyond the mist

but they are

still there

waiting

watching

knowing

knowing what you have

and willing that you use it

more than they did

a stronger

cycle

each

time. -----

Tower of fear

each level

trepidation

caution

reluctance

terror

trauma

disbelief

in and out

of the elevator

we travel

up and down

getting caught

between floors

pressing the help button

but succumbing

to panic

and claustrophobia

while we wait

to escape

to be rescued

tower of fear

we forget

we are not

prisoners locked in

we can get

to the roof

and choose

to jump and fly

perhaps reaching

unknown heights

or we can

get to the bottom floor

and simply walk

out of the door

perception

programming

and people

lock us in the

tower of fear. -----

Duality

opposites

swinging from

one end of

the scale

to the next

up and down

like a seesaw

hitting the ground

with a hard thump

then being

flung so high

in the air

my roots disconnect

I don't feel free

like I'm flying high

I'm held

motionless

in endless

boundless

space

tired or hyper

happy or sad

morose or ecstatic

busy or lazy

fast or slow

darting from one

thing to the next

or simply

not being able

to move

slow exhale

control

becoming aware

able to name it

recognising

accepting

first steps

out of here. -----

I don't know

what I'm doing

I want to break

from the program

but it's scary

unknown

untried

untested

the program

keeps me safe

I know what

to expect

but I know

it's a lie

a cover up

of me

hiding away

unseen

but felt

felt so strongly

yearning to be

free

liberated

empowered

once you know

it's a lie

you can't unknow that

you've glimpsed

the truth

now it is

the actual reality

not the illusion

the lie. -----

The return

just when you think

you're all that

all grown

big and bad

know it all

back it comes

that little voice

triggering that

yearning for approval

wanting them to

say yes

like it

tell you

you're great

the scared

little voice

scared to hear

no

it's rubbish

don't like it

reassure the voice

it's okay

you don't know any better

whisper all you

like

spray your

what ifs

across the skies

I spotted you

I paused

I listened

and I still

saw the new

truth

and did what

I chose

to serve

my reality. -----

WISDOM

Who told you

that you needed

all these things to

be complete

be accepted

approved of

celebrated

loved

What put those

ideas in

your mind

your heart

your programme

Go deeper

to the

depths of

your soul

your quest

for the truth

the reality

will reveal

that you have

been duped

misled

misguided

misinformed

like a seed

in the ground

you have all

that you need

will know all

you need to

know

in the fullness of time

write your own story

follow your own script

self-validate

self-approve

self-accept

here's to your victory celebration. -----

Look inside

Take a peak

What brings you joy?

What do you seek?

Unplug for a while

Ponder your desire

Delve into the shadows

Really bring the fire

It may take time

To find that flame

Of the light within

Do not be tame

Unleash the hidden

Revealing you

This world craves it

Time to live true. -----

I got swept away

The tides of the every day

Took me away from my shore

My grounding, my base

My own private space

Of me

They left behind

The manufactured one

The programmed one

The one who lacked light

From moon or sun

I have forgotten my rescue

My lifeboat and jacket

The tools I use to allow me

To walk

To be just free

But I did not drown

I returned, healed and cleansed

And replaced my crown

Remembering who I am. -----

Take a breath

Empowered

Showered with grace

Cloaked in courage

Bursting with joy

Swimming in peace

Liberated

Living

Living

Living

Space is freedom. -----

I did not want to let go

Say goodbye

I wanted her to stay

That familiar part of me

She'd always been there

Seeing the world through clouds

Changing unclear uncertain

Without real clarity or truth

But she was secure

Predictable repeating patterns

I was afraid to let her go

How would I know what was coming

I wiped the smoke from my eyes

Saw clearly

Released the illusion

Remembered who I was

Why I was here

Courage reigned

Wisdom ruled

Enlightenment had landed

I had much to do

She had to leave

She had had her time

Served her purpose

No fear

She will be transformed transmuted

She would make room for bigger and better

Brighter

Lighter

Purposeful

I thanked her

Hugged her

We parted smiling

I released her from her shackles

And readjusted my crown

Sat on my throne

And saw my queendom

Held it close in peace and joy

Home again

Always complete. -----

She lingered

And hovered

Like a wisp of something long forgotten

A vague memory

A faded feeling

But she lingered

Reminiscent of times past

A past version of me

We had parted

Moved on

And yet she lingered

Her scent stronger at times

At times barely a whiff

She had been part of me

And me of her

Ever a part of each other

Lingering. -----

Take it steady

be at ease

ready to forgive

take a breath

soothe your soul

ready to receive

take a look at the incredible you

ready to step out

and amaze. -----

Caring for self

Know self

What is your truth

Your true self

Know reality

Look with the innocence of a child

See with clear eyes

See yourself

Honour and nurture

The job of a lifetime. -----

What comes forth

When you close your eyes

Use your super lens

To survey your inner world

What comes forth

When you mute the sounds

Honing in on self

To hear your truth

What comes forth

When you hold your boundaries

Fortify the Citadel

Prioritise your needs

What comes forth

When you shake off the vibes

Deflect the energy

To honour your vibration

What comes forth

The truth revealed

The identity remembered

The courage regained

The vision manifested

Freedom Power Clarity

Come forth. -----

Let it out

let it up

whatever you are

denying

pushing down

ignoring

shackling

restricting

ignoring

find the key

unlock it

or it will

find a way

to be free

no matter how

better on your terms

release it

it does not want to

stay captured

like you

it wants

to be free. -----

Who are you talking to?

Don't know, label fell off

how many labels do you wear

you can be so covered in labels

you disappear from sight

hidden beneath labels

labels placed on you

by you

by others

lose the labels

find yourself

peel it off slowly

or rip it off quick

whichever

remove them

let the true self

Emerge. -----

Passive and kind

so meek and mild

things passing over me

as a child

but they didn't pass over

they clung to my soul

absorbed and assimilated

just filling a hole

until the space stretched

and could handle no more

it kept changing shape

making my soul sore

a spark came alight

the fire within burned

fed by word and expectations

energy rumbled and turned

nuclear in nature

discomfort in form

ready for release

unleash the storm

no more holding on

or down or in

dropping the mask

shedding the skin

time to emerge

what's been growing inside

expose my truth

and no longer hide. -----

I think that

I think maybe

I think

there you go

thinking again

you already know

the answers are

accessible to you

deep within

pause breathe in

pause breathe out

release relax focus

if you knew the answer

what would it be?

trust your intuition. -----

They made it look easy

the trees

change happens gracefully

the energy spent in growth

of deep green leaves

luscious fruits

fades in time

the fruit drops

the leaves change colour

and the trees let it happen

no complacency

no mourning

no gripping or hoarding

even when the leaves fall

trees shed no tears

because they know

it's part of a cycle

it has to happen

for life to continue

for seeds to grow

for buds to emerge

for nature to repeat

they make it look so easy

the trees. -----

Relax

is not the absence

of activity

rest

is not the

cessation of work

the whirring mind

planning and reviewing

the onslaught of

stimulation

from social media news

social expectations

not relaxing

or resting

is it so hard to stop

it's really

only a pause

because we'll return to

it again

relaxation and resting

please don't be a vague memory. -----

How do you choose

to live your life?

there is banging

a tin cup

and then there is

music

music

any way you want to

hear it

live it

feel it

express it

let your life

be like music

and put down

the tin cup. -----

I see the pictures

a kaleidoscope

of memories

flickering film

distorted sound

white noise

I breathe

tune out the distraction

tune in

gently twisting the dial

events experiences endless

fails

have obscured the pictures

I breathe

tune out tune in

to restore those pictures

in 4HD

because they are

a part of me

reclaimed. -----

Everyone talks about

the tiny acorn

growing into the

huge massive oak

like it happens with

a wave of a wand

no one mentions

the struggle

to set down

roots

the strain to push

through the Earth

to seek out the

Sun

to reach for the

water

above and below

to breathe in and out

to seek the community

of those the same

or different

to keep going

when a branch is broken

to stretch to unfurl

a leaf

to nurture the acorns

then watch them fall

land where they lay

picked up kicked

trodden on

planted nurtured

not knowing

to begin the cycle

again. -----

Expansion

moving beyond

the illusion of limits

the lies

of false faces

personas

performances

expansion

growing out

yet always

staying connected

to centre

to source

your core stretches

out

shines brighter

comes into being. -----

That fizz

that bubble

electrical excitement

when there is

opportunity

potential

long-held

dreams coming true

the delight in

your eyes

sparkle in your belly

zip in your step

That blow

that bomb

total destruction

when plans are

slashed

serial killer style

dreams demolished

crumbled

to dust

the cave

in your eyes

endlessly empty

The spectrum

of emotions

the not so smoothly

undulating

journeys of life

adventures of the soul

ever turning

wheel of fortune

quill of destiny

writing pages

of change

we share this

the experience

of being here

separate

but one. -----

SUN

Never mind about the laws of the courts, edicts and decrees set down by kings or the laws of any institutions. The law of nature rules all and nature says the sun will always shine on another day. It does not care what the previous day was like or indeed the dark night before; the sun will rise.

And so I too rise with it.

This section charts the beginning; a genesis; the seed of a star holding infinite potential. Ready.

Heru Sa Aakhut: one whose courage comes from Divine knowledge and the Light of God.

Warrior. Wisdom. Sun.

The brightest light.

Glowing orb

peering above

the pastel horizon.

Tentatively stretching out

glowing rays

of warmth

and a deep seated

passion about living. -----

Heart pounding

Eyes lit up

Expanded and bright

No longer in fear

Or doubt

Or fright

The excitement

Of newness

Of taking a risk

Allowing yourself

To be

Lovingly kissed

By joy

And delight

So many things bright

Now you are living

Your truth

Your wholeness

Your right. -----

Wings unfurled

Outstretched

Liberated

And flying

Soaring towards

The heavens

The way I am

Allows me

Permission

To climb free

Basking in power

In joy

In freedom

In truth

In love

The way I am

Divine. -----

Everything is heightened

Today

I stand firm and rooted

In my power

My grace and love

Flows out into the universe

Amongst the stars

Reflecting all sources of light

And providing a beacon

For those whose time it is

To be illuminated

In light

In light

In light. -----

Unleashed

Unbound

Unshackled

Released from the prison

Of her mind

Of her programming

Of what she had been shown

The energy stored within

Sparkles, crackles

Ready to ignite

Explode

A blinding light

And power

Her own power

Fuelled by self-love

Wisdom

Truth

A source of inspiration

Re-enters the world

And lightens the universe. -----

There's a lightness

To your step now

Confidence

And control

You meet a stranger

With a kind smile

Without breaking stride

Or looking back

Or worrying about

How you were

Perceived

In that situation

There's a lightness

To your step now

As you engage

With the world

On your terms

Not a work in progress

So totally

Already complete

And unashamedly

Ever evolving

Stepping lightly

And skipping

Into joy. -----

Grounded

And rooted

Stable

Anchored

But no longer

Stuck

Or still

Or frozen

In fear

And doubt

And regret

A strong foundation

An established trunk

Branches that

Can bend

If they break

There are more

The leaves fall

Tears may fall

There may be barren times

But you are assured

You know

Buds will return

Flowers will bloom

Fruits will grow

Again

They always do

Rebirth

Transformation

Ever cycling. -----

An exhale

As you release the cords that bind you

Deep breath in

As you fully realise the capacity of your lungs

In and out

Fully, easily, without constriction

Brilliance

As you slip off the blindfold you've been wearing

Blinking

As you see the world with new eyes

Taking in the glory

The vibrating life in everything

Calm in the body

As you relax your shoulders

Unclench your jaw

As you realise you can let go

Relinquish the tension, the strain

And move fluidly, fully and fearlessly

Through life. -----

Phoenix rising

Flames flickering

Fan those flames

Create that inferno

That desire

To be

To expand

Take up space

Shine

Shout

Smile

Laugh

Live

Out of the ashes

You will always arise

Again

Fire. -----

Take a glance

Back over your shoulder

Look how far you have come

Look how high up you are

See the view

Take it all in

You made it

You know

You feel it

That joy

The ecstasy of being

Doing the thing that

Has you smiling and laughing

And excited

And hungry for more

And wanting to tell everyone

And share

The fact

You have found

The holy grail

Of you

And loving you

Gratitude abound

Peace throughout

Joy overflowing

All hail the light. -----

SPOKEN WORD

All eyes on me

All eyes on me.

No, that's why I wanted to stay small.

That's why I didn't want to shine my light.

I didn't want all eyes on me

looking and prying and seeing

being the centre of attention

stood in the spotlight.

I know that I had a light to shine

maybe too bright for some,

maybe I would outshine, everyone.

All eyes on me.

No, what if they see

the darkness within

deep, underneath my skin.

Would they be scared?

Would they take flight?

Seeing the truth in the depths of the night.

All eyes on me

No, I don't want them to see

the darkness, the fear, the worry.

But beyond that,

the spark, of light,

of flame, ready to ignite,

ignited, flickering.

Just in need of

air.

The air would make it

go into a roaring fire.

Maybe that would consume others.

Maybe it would consume myself.

And so I dim my light.

I stay in the corner

All eyes on me.

No, not tonight. -----

Flagged

It started off as that tiny speck,

that red petal on the wind

in the corner of my eye

I ignored it and carried on.

I saw the red again, a handkerchief dropped on the ground.

I walked passed, ignored it, it wasn't mine.

It wasn't for me. I was fine.

I saw a red petal again.

Wasn't for me, I ignored it.

Was I blind?

Could I not see?

Everything was fine between you and me?

Everything was fine.

The scarlet that I see

is the redness of your rage.

When you hit me, you strike me with your hands.

You pummel me with your words.

You smash me when you ignore me,

when you withhold your emotions.

And yet I still can't see, the red petal,

the red handkerchief.

Was that the crimson of my blood?

The redness of your eyes

bloodshot while you rant and stamp.

And I cower in a corner,

but it was fine.

It wouldn't happen to me.

It was only

temporary.

The redness, I just could not see.

I had on my blindfold.

My senses were muffled.

I could not hear,

I could not see.

If only I could remove the blindfold.

Then I would notice the red flag that had been torn

and braided

fashioned into a rope

that I was hanging from

that red flag.

I did not see

now strangling me.

If only I could remove the blindfold and see,

I could release myself.

It was strangling me

that red rope

from the red flag.

I did not see. -----

Shifting

I walked and I saw the brown leaves on the ground.

Was it autumn?

I could see the tiny green shoots pushing through.

Was that signs of spring?

I looked up to the skies, so blue,

the clouds moving slowly,

the trees, their branches bare,

like it was winter.

The sun

so bright a summer sun

yet it felt so cold.

It was that time of in-between

like twilight.

When you cannot see clearly

you don't know whether you are in the future

or in the past, or right here in the present.

It's ever shifting.

You see sometimes, you might feel stuck.

You can't move because you can't decide where you need to be;

between seasons, between times

you know that there are always changes.

And sometimes the changes are swift and your head spins around

and it's dizzying.

And sometimes the changes are slow.

And you wonder how you can manage to stay the course

in this in-between time,

the twilight time,

as you mull over what had gone before

you worry about what will come

and you miss what is in the present,

never mind about what you have done.

What you wish to happen.

Stay present in the

in-between.

You'll see what you need to see in that special place.

The twilight,

the shifting seasons,

the in-between. -----

Nature

Nature's greatest promise

a contract

a renewal

ever binding

a promise of spring

of change

a renewal of growth

of always having the opportunity

to do it again

to do it differently

to see

to feel

to know

that it will come round again

differently

and it'll be fine. -----

Hawthorn

I am life.

I am life itself.

I see all, I grow, I stretch, I came from a seed and exploded into life.

Fresh and vibrant. My leaves unfurling to the sun.

My blossoms blooming like explosions, fireworks, pretty white flowers.

Pretty white flowers, that can adorn the most beautiful women. A crown upon the Empress' head.

White stars that you can see in the daylight, on a carpet of green.

My trunk is gnarled as it turns and it rides and it works its way round, twisting, always moving forward against all the odds.

Having that strength. I am Hawthorne. I am Hawthorne. I am Hawthorne.

My limbs stretch outwards reaching for the

sunlight, my roots stretch downwards reaching for the other roots.

Come take my pretty flowers.

Make a crown, adorn yourself, walk tall as the Queen, as the Empress that you are.

Sit on your throne of comfort, nurture the land, the land will nurture you.

I am Hawthorne.

I work against the odds.

Parts of me may seem unseemly. They may seem not so pretty, but parts of me are.

I am light, I am life. I erupted from a seed. I stretched upwards to the heavens.

I dug deep down to the core of the earth.

My leaves unfurl. Light green to dark green, energized by the sun.

My flowers sparkle brightly like diamonds in a crown. Your crown, Empress. Your crown,

Queen. Your crown.

Walk tall. Take your place.

Stand high, root deep, expand and be. -----

Trees

They call to me, the trees.

High in the sky, the branches waving,

calling to me, beckoning me near to

come and listen,

to hear what they have to say.

The messages that they have

from their deep knowledge.

Knowledge that comes from

the knowing of being here,

being here for all time, for every time, everywhere.

Their roots dig deep, deep down,

connecting; connecting with everything.

The trees, they know all.

They beckon to me, the trees.

They say, come, come and hear.

Listen, listen to the messages

and the rustle of the leaves

and the sway of our branches.

Listen to what we say.

When you touch the rough bark of our trunk:

the strength of our trunk

that holds us steady;

that holds the branches reaching towards the heavens;

reaching towards and connecting the other realms, touching the clouds, the great sky.

The trunk that connects to the roots, again, reaching out.

The trees they envelope everything.

They're here always.

Will you listen? -----

Sunshine

Ooh, the sunshine.

Ah, the warmth, the joy, the vibration, the light, the gladness, the happiness, the sunshine.

We don't get enough of it, not here anyway.

We always crave more and when we crave more and more, do we get more?

Because we're not always craving more.

We complain.

"It's too hot."

"Where's the air conditioning?"

"Oh, the sun's in my eyes."

"Oh, I want to walk in the shade."

So strange are we.

We want the sunshine and when we get it,

we complain.

How can that be?

When we truly crave something and open up

ourselves to express it and receive it,

we gain more.

Are we really shut off to the sunshine?

Are we shut off to the light?

Is it something that we think we should have?

Do we think we deserve it? Is that the issue?

The sunshine brings light and life

and laughter and flow and joy and all good things.

But do we believe we deserve it?

Think deeply. Are we open to receiving?

Are we open to the light? The light that is a reflection of us?

The light that is part of our source. The sunshine. Think on it.

Do we want the sunshine? -----

Weeds

Weeds. Who decides what a weed is?

Isn't a weed of flower? Isn't a weed a plant?

Doesn't a weed deserve

the same amount of light and water and food and love?

Who decides what a weed is?

Weeds are frowned upon because they go against the norm.

They don't grow in neat little rows.

They appear out of nowhere.

They're inconvenient. They shake things up.

They spread and they grow wild and they cannot be controlled, they're strong, resilient, they burst forth through the concrete, disrupting things.

Who decides what a weed is?

Could a rose be a weed? In a different situation, under different circumstances?

Could a tulip be a weed? In a different

situation, under different circumstances?

Who decides what a weed is?

They call you weedy and weak. A weed isn't weak.

Something that bursts through concrete cannot be weak.

Do not fear when they call you weedy, stand tall and proud.

What it is to be a weed.

Weeds feed the insects.

Weeds are part of the world.

They play their part.

They feed what needs to be fed.

They bring forth what needs to be brought forth.

Who decides what a weed is? Do you decide what a weed is?

Are you a weed? Am I a weed?

Would you want to be a weed?

Why not? -----

Coming for you

You're so kind. Oh, you are so good. You're so nice. Thank you.

These are the things that I often hear. Yeah, they sound nice.

They made me feel good for a hot minute.

I mean, I have tolerance; tenacity.

You could say that they're superpowers, but to me they're more like kryptonite.

They weaken me.

People take advantage of that

because I have tenacity.

It means I can put up with stuff

again and again and again and again for longer and longer and longer.

Because I have that tenacity means I can go on and on just like a Duracell battery.

Because sometimes I lack boundaries.

So people trample their way, steal my energy;

take and take and leave nothing for me.

Hmm.

These things aren't super powers.

Are they a blessing or a curse?

I have to find a way to make them work for me.

Trust

Trust in me.

That's what I need to develop, so I can see the true reality.

I can put up my boundaries. Let in who I want.

It's my choice. Choose my own superpowers.

Bring them forth whenever I need.

Keep myself safe and sane.

Welcome in the kind of energy that I would like to see.

And in that way I can truly become me.

Lift my voice, Drop the programs.

Grow into my authenticity.

Don't worry.

I'm coming for you.

This is just a first draft.

This is version 2.0.

Wait till you see the finished version,

of me. -----

Speak

I lost my voice

Or did I lose it or did I give it away?

I don't want to admit that I gave it away

because if I gave away something that was mine

along comes those feelings of shame and guilt.

And why didn't I keep it and why didn't I look after it?

And I was gifted with it. Why didn't I use it?

Did I lose my voice? Did I give it away?

Regardless, I didn't have my voice.

I was taught to stay quiet, seen and not heard.

Looking pretty, looking good.

Never saying a word really.

So I didn't get the practice of using my

voice.

I might have put my voice across through, my work, through my study,

maybe through the way I present myself,

but I was never really using my voice.

It's taken me a while to remember that I have a voice, that I can use it.

It's not necessarily safe to use my voice all the time,

but it's certainly less dangerous.

Or maybe it's because I've become more courageous.

I'm inspired by those that use their voice.

But inspiration. It's just looking and admiring.

What am I going to do with that inspiration?

I choose now to use my voice. I want to be remembered for my voice.

I see those younger ones coming up with

bravery using their voice and they inspire me.

I see those before me who have used their voice and they inspire me.

So I choose now to use my voice. -----

WARRIOR WISDOM SUN

ACKNOWLEDGEMENTS

Many thanks to all my teachers, from childhood to now.

Cousin Ju – for always being there

Tarze Edwards – Small: my best friend and my number one cheerleader

Andrew Stockhausen (my oldest friend) – for accepting me and celebrating me just as I am

Michael Small – when others are lost you remain; a steadfast brother

Samira Belrhazi – for helping to unlock the real me

Karen, Claire, Chelsey and Wendy – this book would have taken a lot longer to be completed and reach the light of day without you.

The next generation (in age order): Nyle, Kamau, Xsienna, Kyram, Adina, Usert, Raniya, Rakaii – so you have something concrete as well as the memories.

"Always look for the truth in a situation. Stay curious."

WARRIOR WISDOM SUN

Life gets in the way

That's what we

Always say

When we do not

Reach a dream

And our passions

Always seem

So far beyond our reach

If someone could

Just teach

Us we do have a choice

To just be and

Own our voice

We would take

A risk and see

Our dreams

Could be reality.

WARRIOR WISDOM SUN

ABOUT THE AUTHOR

Having taught in education for over twenty-five years, Sarah currently works in an advisory capacity in her home city of Nottingham, England.

In later years, Sarah discovered the ancient art of acupuncture and is now a fully qualified practitioner. Helping others (both physically and mentally) led to the realisation that it was time to slow down and focus upon her own internal thoughts and emotional well-being. Having always fostered her creative side, through the lens of dance and musicality, Sarah - being an avid reader- has now taken her first foray into the art of the written word.

Acknowledging the personal healing power of her own writing journey inspired Sarah to share her work in the hope that her words may provide comfort, connection, acceptance, and strength in her readers.

Instagram: @writingforlight

Printed in Great Britain
by Amazon